The
Carpenter's
Son

CARLYLE MARNEY

The
Carpenter's
Son

CHANTICLEER PUBLISHING COMPANY, Inc.
WAKE FOREST, NORTH CAROLINA

THE CARPENTER'S SON

Chanticleer Publishing Company, Inc.
Box 501
Wake Forest, North Carolina 27587

The Perkins Sermons

In appreciative regard
for the hearing given these essays
by the citizens of her city, this
twenty-second series of morning lectures
on the J. J. Perkins Lectureship
is dedicated to

LOIS PERKINS

AND HER FAMILY

Introduction

● THAT IRRESISTIBLY WINSOME AND GRA-
cious man, J. G. Hughes, who taught me all I
know about true pastors, always seemed to me to
preach and teach as if he had just heard from
the Almighty. I knew of his discouraged times
and tasted the loneliness some days, but when
he came out on Sundays he seemed very sure
of the Eternal.

For years I longed and felt after this certainty
for myself. But there was a contrary testimony.
And it was mostly when I preached something
I was afraid to preach that I had any assurance
at all. Essentially I wanted to be loved, I sup-
pose, but most of all I wanted what Hughes
seemed to feel. And so, for years at a time,
my preaching was on themes that threatened
me, frightened me, but God did not come,
except rarely in some ego afterglow or in the
act of delivery.

Now, in my maturer years, I am reasonably sure that sermons are seldom, if ever, God-breathed. He really does leave it to us—he does not write it. It can be trash or piffle or heresy or stupid for all of him. He is *Silence*. (Irenaeus calls this, too, after Ignatius.) Darwin said God had not bothered him for twenty years and Ruskin said the earlier visions went silent. Except for my colleagues and friends and family and books I am on my own—most days. My utterances are not sacred even to me. And what does this mean?

It must mean God has quit talking. I am suspicious and frightened of, even angered by, those men to whom God talks so freely. Why would God talk to those glib ones and not to me? I am a veteran now: of pastorates where poverty pinched your nose with its odors, where soap was a luxury and children lived like rats under houses and smelled like urinals when you lifted them; of pastorates where ignorance and bigotry were worn like badges and race hatred was both milk and bread; of pastorates where all education was for killing with knives or guns and where ten thousand of the enemy were prisoners of war across the street; where twenty thousand university students left the town no better than they found it, except for

8

scars; and now in plusher circumstances, but just as needy and scarred, even more spoiled and self-centered. In none of this, these years since 1941, has God said anything NEW that I could hear.

> Is it not because he has nothing to say
> until we have heard his last word?

We all remember how precious is the word of a loved one when it turns out to have been his *last* word. Letters are treasured and memorized. Words meant casually are given incredible meaning. Time and again the church grasps for some new word, but we are always driven to the last thing God said for sure.

This is what the New Testament is about: the last things they said God said. Looking back over their shoulder for a time when God was alive they remembered he made a Testamentary—a Covenant—a Last Will and Deed —a Word—the last thing God said was Jesus who is the Christ. You may as well admit it. After Jesus comes on stage the subject of Holy Scripture is the Christ. This is what it means to call him the Word of God.

> God had said other words, but
> not lately, and *Talmud* is but embroidery on a word already spoken.

9

So is Christian history just embroidery. Church history has been our hearing and mishearing and refusing to hear the Son. And all our "denominations" represent some mishearing of God's last word. Even our precious unheard Holy Spirit, since the fourth century *filioque* clause was added, is heard to speak through and from the Son for it was of the Son that the Holy Spirit reminded us, taught us, rebuked us, and caused us to remember. Every distorted record is a distortion of the Son—for this is the last word from God we have heard.

THEOLOGY never unpacks its bag and stays. This is why no theology can be God's last word. There is, they say, a massive revolt against Karl Barth on the Continent. I am sorry for I wish he could have stayed longer and finished his cathedral. It's a lovely place to go—and of all who write he has been most lovable and dear. But none can stay. The young ones have run past Bultmann, now an incident in their hermeneutical past. And having taken their very ability to breathe modern air from Tillich, they say (in a couple of paragraphs) that the old master has had his day. They let the great German ease them down from their idealistic heritage to the tragic realism that is underneath, use the critical realism of Reinhold Niebuhr as if they had spawned it, fall over in the existentialist sprawl where World War II left all of us, and announce that "God is dead" as a new theology.

It is neither new nor theology. Most of us have known it since Feuerbach—and are grateful that Nietzsche softens it greatly, even weeps that we killed him—but those of us who felt this have generally said it more modestly and a day at a time:

God is dead—*for me*—we sometimes have to say in the silence: but we do not thereby mean to pronounce his demise over the whole universe!

And we weep over it; there is a sob if we say it aloud, because, as Blake Smith puts it, some of us have been on the Emmaus Road and "had hoped." To say that God is dead is not a good way to say our situation—though the end effect is the same. We have always been responsible—with the Son.

It seems, then, less presumptuous, more honest and more Christian to say, with Buber, *the eclipse of God.* For the God who does not talk to men in the sacred or secular cities of our time may very well be the God who does not talk because he has *said* it. He has no more to say until the Son is heard.

The New Testament epistles hang the goal there plainly before our eyes. We are to come into the likeness of the Son! Till then God will not need to speak again.

When God says "man" he means "Jesus the Christ"—not "Adam." This much at least we keep from Barth. And the young American Turks in theology are concerned with the great humanity of the Son, and this is fine—provided we remember.

Provided we remember that we cannot talk of a Christ who matters without talking of the one obsession of his life—to know and do the Father's Will.

The Christian churches keep trying to add words. Now the *New Yorker* has confirmed the last of the series in a classic cartoon:

Relate to thy Neighbor!

Words, even the most recent, will not do it. Words can only rise from the Word; church can only result from meeting; and theology must always be a memory first of all. God is where the Son has happened among us and the Word still precedes our words.

Contents

I

The
Man for
Others

AND coming to his own country he taught them in their synagogue, so that they were astonished, and said, "Where did this man get this wisdom and these mighty works? Is not this the carpenter's son? Is not his mother called Mary? And are not his brothers James and Joseph and Simon and Judas? And are not all his sisters with us? Where then did this man get all this?" And they took offense at him. But Jesus said to them, "A prophet is not without honor except in his own country and in his own house." And he did not do many mighty works there, because of their unbelief.

—MATTHEW 13:54-58

● THE FIRST QUESTION, AND IN SOME SENSE
the only question, concerning Jesus is "Who is
he?" It is almost incredible that two thousand
years later it should be still a question. All the
wrong answers are still alive. We are nearly all
victims of one docetic explanation of his divinity, or another. But this divinity bit was not yet
a problem when they first asked—"Is this not
the carpenter's son?"

The question means that something unexpec-
ted has come from him. It means "Who expects
this of a carpenter's son?" And what is expected
of a carpenter's son? Just this: He shall look
and act and be more like the carpenter than
anyone else!

This must seem an innocuous sort of text
for a modern audience—so far removed from

being affected by any answer to the question. What difference does it make that he was or was not the carpenter's son? On the face of it, it makes a great deal of difference. This was no debate over his origins. 'Tis a rhetorical question only—and meant to be answered, "Yes, he is the carpenter's son. Yes, he is what he seems to be." "What he appeared to be, that he was," Irenaeus would claim a century later. No question of a "virgin" birth here; no angels fluttering wreaths over rooftops; no advent signs and voices here; it doesn't enter their minds that he could be really anyone else than the brother of his brothers. Rather, here is a man acting contrary to their notion of his heritage, that is all. If he is the carpenter's son, why is he not content to act as the carpenter's son? And why they have asked the question at all becomes the real story.

I

HERE is a man who so far transcends what is expected of a mere man that the only way they could account for him was by questioning the mereness of his manhood. It is so much easier for us all if he is of extraordinary lineage. The proper sons of genius who are themselves geniuses do not upset us. We are not astounded by princes who turn out to be worthy sons of worthy kings. It's these sons of blacksmiths who measure too far out beyond the ordinary that upset us. Why? Because these carpenter's sons, if they really are, keep saying that the extraordinary is in the reach of us all. And this convicts us, embarrasses us, confounds us—if all *he* had is *our* potential! So we say of these full-men: extraordinary sources, strength, power is explained by extraordinary parentage, birth, lineage. We become Docetists about our full-men and say they are not really men. This makes it so much easier for us all.

For two thousand years the claim that he is divine has threatened the manhood of the Christ. But whatever divinity means it cannot deny his utter manhood and leave an incarnation. Whatever God had to do with here, he was a man. Yet I do not wonder that they questioned. It *was* so out of the ordinary: a peasant with two thousand years of wisdom pushing him; all the insights of a vast heritage inducted in half-a-dozen statements; an at-homeness in liturgy and legend, a primitive savant, a finished rabban, a Ph.D. in a hut! And more, and worse, he displays such an easy familiarity with our ethereals and eternals. Is this not the car-

19

penter's son? Is this not within the grasp of everyone? Perhaps not; but more than we have grasped is within our untouched potential.

The question I have caricatured and the christological questions I have ignored permeate this chapters 13-16 layer of Matthew's Gospel. The section reaches its climax in Messiah's own question, "Who do *you* say that I am?" All these questions get no answer here or now. But any answer offered to any of these questions about Christ's identity must include a manhood available to us all or his was a pointless demonstration. Even his death had to offer a triumph within our reach or his was a pointless suffering. Whoever he is, he became a man under the terms of manhood available to all.

You have a heritage available to you, but of it we are mostly ignorant men, wrapped up in our postadolescent identity crises and the creation of new layers of lacquer for our self-images. You have an education for growth available to you, but by your fortieth year you will be men whose growth has largely stopped. The books, the memories and wisdoms, joys, insights, values, and victories you will have glossed over and left behind you, mostly unread, unknown, unused. It may never really enter your mind that a private Reformation for humanity could

begin where you are, even as a public one
began that day in Nazareth. In the main those
who keep any institutional religious affiliation
at all limp periodically into secluded little cor-
ners to try to keep a day that never was—and
for such there is no fulfillment. There is simply
nothing at stake.

Downtown, the pressures of the competitive
business world will crush you until you hardly
see the extent of your slavery, until your tanned
and eager spirits have become a faceless but
still eager conforming flatulence in the world
of Moloch. You will be retired after your first
heart attack, eventually die and be buried, but,
like Willie Loman in *Death of a Salesman,* you
will never have discovered who you are.

Or, the patterns of the legal profession will
distort your soul. Until and unless you learn of
a higher potential of *agape* and *charis,* uncon-
ditioned love and free grace, available even in
men, you will go on defining your own good
with your own *ratio,* worshiping the creature
more than the creator, turning God's truth into
a private lie, still adoring the great god *Prece-
dent* under the ethic of Thrasymachus and
Machiavelli (might makes right, if you can, do);
eventually you will go away, never learning of
the rooms you had upstairs but never visited.

21

The access roads to a professional ministry are no better. Here, too, we learn to want things, posts, and places, and life can revolve around a man in the ministry as senselessly, more senselessly, than any place I know.

Among students? The frightening matter of this culture-wide rejection of our humanity (which is a rejection of your own potential) means that many would be lost in the banquet of learning offered in any university. We can no longer count on your *motivation* for BECOMING. There seems to be almost nothing some of you want that you haven't already *got*. So, Ivy-League urbanity, or coast-league vacuity, or bush-league provincialism become a pasture in which you loll in white-bucked, red-soled desuetude. You may never know the redder law of cosmic becoming until your exposure to meaning and relevance is dissipated and you just disappear into the facelessness, as *Bom* or *Pim* in Samuel Beckett's *How It Is*.

And here we see many of you no more. The appeals of a sensate culture smother you in the odors of your own flesh until the arts of cosmetology and the science of geriatrics meet you in the technique of embalming and you have to endure the curse of remaining as you are— for time gets everything. You are caught in an

unrealized potential, trapped like the young
Augustine in the birdlime of your own nest
by your own sprouting feathers; racked in between your bridge tournaments, your golf after-
noons, and your five o'clock breaks.

II

WHO will call us to our unachieved manhood
if Messiah cannot? Who will spark us, strike
us to the heart with a realization that the
kingdom of heaven on earth is really within
our reach? Who will help us reach a human
potential we can't even imagine? Who will
plan and want and do grandly enough to make
us worthy of the journey we have started? Who
will convince us that we simply do not have
to die as we are; fat, flaccid, unrealized, and
ignorant men?

This was the threat to those citizens of ancient
Nazareth that rested in that carpenter's son.
He represented an unrealized manhood available to us all. He calls us not yet to a divinity;
there is a manhood implicit in us all to be
realized first. This is his meaning as the Man
for Others. This is the challenge to become,
like him, the emptied man.

The meaning of his sheer manhood is that

23

there is a potential in our very manhood enough to make the angels jealous and the heavens to sing, if only we would grasp it. The meaning of his use of the tools available in his own culture is that with tools already in hand and by light we already have we could drive heartlessness from the earth. There are in the culture of the Western world already the tools, techniques, and knowledge to get at the cultural and character causes of our poverty, the insight to destroy our attachment to false goods and gods, and the power to curse and turn from our own complacency. We have the strength already to make a toughened, disciplined, hardened youth. We have enough work in every village to save all our adults from boredom, ennui, and desuetude. We even have a dream big enough to die in and for. And who can set it off and call us forth if this fairest one we ever saw, the Carpenter's Son, cannot?

Jules Henry says that we serve our drives in our work and our values somewhere else. I think not. Our drives have become our values and our zeal is to see to their satisfaction. Our drives exist to assure us we are alive! As long as appetite is keen, sex urges are regular, curiosity is beckoning, and travel is possible—as long as we can see, feel, taste, hear, and smell—and as long as all body urges work, we know we are still alive and our work is to feed these urges we value as barometers of our existence. This is how we become such sensualists, lost in our own body processes. This is what work is *for;* to keep us occupied during the recuperating span of our fleshly drives so that we can recover our juices for a new "relaxation." This is what sleep is for—to rest the flesh and brain for a new indulgence. And then, tragic day, something happens to both work and sleep at the same time. They are cut off as servers of our leisure and our drives.

My heart bleeds for those poor senior workers who must face now an annual thirteen-week vacation! With full pay they must live through the terrible hours of a cessation from toil they never have learned how to use. They, mostly, like the rest of us, have worked for the wrong reasons. They, too, have used the earth and its colors, skies, joys, smells, and agonies like any other breeding, fighting, herd-bound animal. There is man-sign everywhere there is filth, disease, damage, and heartbreak. Only here and there can a man stay at home, retired, without losing his mind! And just as there is no boor like the man who has learned to despise the boyhood home that made him, so there is no forgiveness or recovery for a people that have overlooked and ignored the tools and the power of the culture that surrounds them.

As early as 1830 Alexis de Tocqueville saw and said this about us. In the same century Lord Macaulay wrote to a supporter of Jefferson's ideals to say that we were in for terrible trouble as soon as our land resources were occupied because common man cannot be trusted to know his own heritage. Only an aristocracy can help us—only an inbred superior class can prevent it. We must lose here either our liberty or our living.

This is the Tory kind of talk. This is the Burkean philosophy of the old Virginian, Randolph; this is the Southern planter's talk—and it is not so. Granted that Tom Jefferson was incredibly naïve about what the common man would do with his education, we do not have to fall for this pessimism about man—as yet. Not so long as we can see the Carpenter's Son, using the tools of his time and place, to carve out, as Man for Others, an attainable place for man.

But who would deny that even now the picture of common man as the great defaulter of a heritage is compounded by all we see, hear, and know? This guilt of serving our animal drivenness, this inability of our children to break the vicious round, this magnification of nursing dependency through grandparental indulgence and interference—all these add up to make a true aristocracy impossible anymore unless it emerges in a whole being saved. For even to this day the rarest human being is that man whose drives serve worthy values.

This is the human Jesus; his drives all serve the One. He is the Collected Man; he is the Gathered Man; he is the man at home in this world. He is free to live for the true, the beautiful, the just, and the holy. He is complete. He is the Carpenter's Son.

III

AND how can this fullness come upon us? In the Nazareth setting, surrounded by villagers who had access to the same cultural sources, Jesus had laid hold of a manhood so astounding as to make them question his lineage. "Is this not the Carpenter's Son? Is he not among his brothers Joseph, Simon, et cetera? And are not his mother and his sisters among us still?"

For this Jesus had an answer: "Who is my family! Who are my sisters and my brothers and my mother? *Those who do the will of my*

Father! These are my mother and my sisters and my brethren!"

You knew already that this humanism bit would run out before we got anywhere, didn't you? It always does. Our humanisms all run out at the edge of death and evil and the exhausting boundary of our inability to do as good as we know. This is a human-boundary situation, as Tillich would call it. At the very lip of the realization of our manhood we fall back into our animal-ness because of a failure of will. This is the edge and the end of all the utopian dreams of history from the Jewish Zion to the Jewish Marx. We run into a failure of will.

Knowledge we ask not—knowledge Thou hast lent,
But, Lord, the will—there lies our bitter need.
　　　　　　　　　　　　—John Drinkwater

Unless some hand beyond us! Without some indispensable conversion of the will!

Here is the secret of the Carpenter's Son. He knows no division of the will. His is an undivided heart. Here before us is Sören Kierkegaard's "Purity of Heart is to will one thing!" In the context of 186 verses of John's Gospel alone the Carpenter's Son is seen to be obsessed by knowing and doing the Father's will. The

Father will supply the will! The will of the Living One engrafts itself upon the desiring heart. His will is for our willing to do his will. The word is Richard Niebuhr's *radical obedience,* the will for which emerges from that radical realization within a radical monotheism of the *Oneness* of things in the Holy One. Is not this heritage available to us? Every day since the "Hear, O Israel, the Lord our God is One" was born this power has been ours, too.

The conversion of the will begins in our *desire.* One has to want this will to do because he wants to be man—not a beast. The hunger is there—given—and if a man wants it fed, if he desires, he can know the conversion of the will. The nature of his relation to the Father's desiring for him is of the nature of response. He is called—he answers. He is summoned—he obeys. In obeying—the will develops. As he matures in choosing-responding-desiring, his will matures, but he always has more light than he has followed. Even the Greeks and the pagans, says John Baillie, know enough to be far better men than they are!"

The goal of our en-manning is to do the Father's will. And as for one who does this, it was enough to get a man called Son of God, in the Hebrew sense of the word. It still is.

29

II
The
Sign of
Jonah

And the Pharisees and Sadducees came, and to test him they asked him to show them a sign from heaven. He answered them, "When it is evening, you say, 'It will be fair weather; for the sky is red.' And in the morning, 'It will be stormy today, for the sky is red and threatening.' You know how to interpret the appearance of the sky, but you cannot interpret the signs of the times. An evil and adulterous generation seeks for a sign, but no sign shall be given to it except the sign of Jonah." So he left them and departed.

—Matthew 16:1-4

● When they pressed him for some magnificent confirmation of their suspicions; when they asked for indubitable evidence that he was more than a carpenter's son; when they crowded around seeking to taunt out of him some affirmation of his more-than-prophetic capacities; when they wished to gouge him to the point that he would rear back and pass a miracle; he said—

You adulterers of a culture and a religion, I'll give you a sign!
　　(As plain as a red sky in the evening
　　As readable as a low'ring sky at dawn.)

　The sign? Old Tecumseh used a comet the British agents had said would cross Alabama when the Five Nations were to be in council. Constantine saw a cross in the sky and had his sergeants carry a banner clear to Mulvian Bridge. Some of the Crusaders followed a goose, and some ran behind Peter the Hermit's mule pulling the sacred hair till the mule was bald behind. William the Conqueror used a handful of English mud. Moses used a stick and some snakes and manna from the bountiful sky, they said. Sherman used the smoke of Atlanta, visible for sixty miles, to keep his exodus of contraband slaves in line. When they pressed the Carpenter's Son for a sign, he said at last:

> I'll give you a sign
> Jonah has been here
> Jonah has come and you cannot hear.

I

EVERYBODY thought of the whale! Even the editors of Matthew's Gospel thought that he meant the fish. And so they made a sign of Resurrection from the vomitus of a troubled fish. But he meant both much more and much, much less than this.

He meant that the only sign of its end a culture can expect is a man who speaks his piece. This is Pericles at Athens; this is Elijah on Carmel; this is Cicero against Catiline; this is Savonarola in Florence, and Churchill addressing the British Parliament, and Dibelius, Lilje, and Niemöller to the Nazis; this is Tom Paine to the New York Tories and Charles Malik to Vishinsky at United Nations General Assembly. It's all the same.

No whale, no miracle, no sizzling sign from the sky. Just a kind of reluctant foreigner speaking his piece. This is always the sign of Jonah.

Nineveh, the boiling pot on Israel's northern flank, the capital of the Assyrian Empire of Sennacherib, required a three-day walk to get downtown. It sprawled across its own landscape like a giant from the sea and represented the power that would swallow the ten tribes of Israel like an octopus. She would withdraw her widespread exploring tentacles only at Jerusalem's outer walls after some calamitous trouble had befallen Sennacherib. Her ten-ton black bulls skipped like rams on the backs of millions of devoted patriots who believed in the Assyrian "genius." And Jonah: reluctant, truculent, unwilling, human, battered, half-digested, ill-willed preacher—walking and crying "Forty days, forty days and Ninevah will be destroyed!" Like

35

George Fox, the Quaker, crying Woe to Lichfield!—and their common theme is *Shūv*, Turn!

Unlike Lichfield, Nineveh did turn, the play says. But history denies it. With the story of more than twenty civilizations history denies that Nineveh turned. She has been an uninhabited heap these 2,700 years and did not turn for long. Neither did Rome, or Persia, or Germany turn. And what sign do we get here? The sign of Jonah, and that is all; all any culture gets as a sign of its end.

Leo X had determined to be a different kind of pope from his predecessor Julius II. Julius, who had himself painted as a warrior with a sword, patron of Michelangelo, was nearer an emperor than a pastor of the pastors of God. But, nevertheless, he would be hard to follow for Rome had bloomed with his largess. Leo, huge, brilliant, elected pope at thirty-seven, helped along by the rumor that he had an incurable fistula, was known as "a library and a museum" in his own person. Born Giovanni de Medici, with all the Medici power to draw upon, he made his rooms a place for artists, sculptors, poets, and crowned their efforts by installing Raphael as his favorite. Under Leo, and the Medici, Rome would at last be fulfilled.

With noted hosts such as Chigi, who threw his silver service into the Tiber after meals (but had nets under water to retrieve his grandiosity), and with buffoons such as Friar Mariano, who could eat four hundred eggs at a sitting, Rome had come into her own. Yet, when Leo X came to sit in the high papal chair under the frieze commissioned by his predecessor, Julius, he probably never looked up to see that above that symbol of every medieval power Michelangelo had put the sign!

The sign of the prophet Jonah!
It is enough to make a man from *any* culture look up and ask, "What heavy, heavy hand hangs over *my* head!" For Jonah has been here, too.

II

SOMETIMES Jonah is a newspaper columnist or an editor, a political candidate, or a visiting evangelist, an economics professor, or an historian. The matter is not that we have no Jonahs. Jonahs are everywhere; most any of us have prophesied with some reluctant call to repent. Indeed there are those who, like Jonah, are aghast when repentance comes, for we had really rather see some of these Ninevehs blow up! The problem is not to find Jonahs. Rather,

37

it is how a church and people and culture should hear its Jonahs. "Men and brethren," they said when Peter had preached, "what shall we do?"

We could turn against religion; that religion which is the end of something instead of the beginning, middle, and end of everything important. We could turn from that prayer wheel of endlessly repeated platitudes which diverts us from a proper work and watch; that religion of lip service to values we do not really serve. (In a recent poll 80 percent claimed the Bible is *the* Book—70 percent had never read it—53 percent could not name Genesis, Exodus, and Leviticus in that order.) We could remove ourselves from those institutional monstrosities which swallow up like Moloch our human responsibilities for being changers-of-the-world. We could renounce the temple-centered and ended repository of hopes that is a dead-end street for any real becoming because it provides no exit into a life of real involvement with any need that matters. We could seek another faith than a religion of easy alignment which lets us live such loosely stewarded lives in the service of such temporary desires. We could begin to deny that federal theology that releases us of any responsibility for our time and state by claiming a sovereignty of God so removed from us that our manhood disappears in puppetry. We could turn against that Protestantism of a pious, upper-class, walled-in, respected, do-nothing status. We could become again a pilgrim people looking for the springtime of the human race instead of bound in this "never-ending winter."

We could, in other words, postpone our reaching for a comfortable and righteous divinity until we realize something of our humanity. We could give the city more cause to ask: "Are they not mere carpenters' sons? How know they these things?" That is to say, *we may be called to turn from a dying religion to a real humanity within our grasp, a kingdom of God within our reach, by frankly using the tools and structures we have to serve in the secular as if it were holy already!*

This was the driving stance of the human, the incredibly human Jesus, who, with tools he took from his own culture, made an exit for humanity through the temple walls of a religion that blocked the way. He drove a coach and horses through those sacred precincts, leaving his hard tracks everywhere, as Dorothy Sayers used to say. "Is he not the carpenter's son?" they queried. Is there not here a manhood available to us all? Who will save us from our fake leisures and the ignorances that distort our lives? Who will begin to ask the questions that goad us to become full-blown sons of carpenters? Who will inspire us to become that rarest human being: the man whose drives serve worthy values? This is the human Jesus, the Jew. His drives all serve the One. He is the collected, the gathered, man—the man at home in the world who is free to live for the true, the beautiful, the just, and the holy—and not for the profitable, the successful, the attractive, and the popular. He is free to serve the completion of our humanity. He is the Carpenter's Son.

III

You who are inclined to do your revolution against religion by simply cursing these walls and stones—this is no proper revolution. It was a revolution against religion that built this place! The proper revolution requires us to take our human powers and our secular connections as redemptive instruments in the service of a holy-secular. And some of this we are seeing:

A family expresses its revolution against tyranny by taking a fourteen-year-old Castrorefugee as its son. A pair revolts against religious intolerance and ignorance by prowling our shelves for the books. A man dressed in the power of much property whispers in the crowd at the door that he has discovered what kind of church God does not want, then uses his strength to demand cleaner rows of tenant housing. An engineer takes on the distribution problems of a Ghana mission where the trouble is how to get 230 volts of electricity along 2,400 feet of wire without turning down the lights in surgery or shutting down the laundry in the orphanage. An eye-surgeon says he will go to West Africa to do that string of operations no one there can do. A local construction expert opens a door in Iran for advance agents of a hospital program. At the coffee-hour someone hands you a check to give a timid Negro beginner his second semester at school. A taxi-franchise owner prowls the back sides of the city looking for half a dozen places to put a house-church and a big-mamma to breed courage and character in the pools of our poverty. Twenty-one people sit around a table asking "for what are we in the world—what is our indispensable service and our irreplaceable function?" The proper revolution may be one woman putting 748 of her hours on a hospital

41

corridor as a volunteer this year. Your proper
revolution may be to become one of the several
hundred who have a private pupil each in the
literacy program. These are all timid evidences
of a spreading revolution and a beginning aware-
ness as to how the secular serves the human in
a holy way. And time would fail if I were to
tell of that day when the chamber of commerce
became, for a moment at least, a temple of the
God who lives, in the service of a suffering race.

IV

But let me give you a caution about joining
the revolt against religion. This can be a
dangerous enterprise. In finding yourself fed up
with the merry-go-round of our religious Vanity
Fairs, in turning your face from the trapeze acts
that have been used to keep you in our pews—
you could find yourself involved with what
God has been doing since that first Isaiah. All
along he has been raising up revolutionaries to
shake up his temples to recover their function
and relation; but this is another topic.

To join this revolution in which God has
been involved may force you to transcend cate-
gories that are precious and shed adjectives
that are welded to your self-image, and this is

42

frightening. Words such as "white" and "Baptist" and "Anglo-Saxon" and the names of your various other sororities begin to drop from your consciousness. To join this revolution could put you on far shores with no decent temples, more "religious" than ever. It might make you use your technical know-how in the secular to serve those you meet in the secular without need of the fake slogans as dead as Main Street and Babbit. It could leave you so bereft of a structured faith you would be forced to find a church in your own house with your own wife. Or even, pray God, it could have the effect of causing you to learn what church is for—to spark your revolt against the bonds of your enslaving religion of mammon or race or status or flesh or whatever lesser god you have loved.

As George Buttrick put it once at Cambridge, you had better be careful coming to church like this. You may have a hand laid on your shoulder to apprehend you for that for which you have already been apprehended by God. A hand that calls you into this revolution may lead you to where you have to become a man for others, too.

When Jonah had made his sign against Nineveh and rested under the gourd vine, it died. Then Jonah cursed the gourd. We didn't set out to make gourds, but trees, planted by the rivers of water, that brings forth her fruit in her season—a different kind of timber. We are to be carpenters' sons involved with a different timber.

III

Who
Do You
Say?

Now when Jesus came into the district of Caesarea Philippi, he asked his disciples, "Who do men say that the Son of man is?" And they said, "Some say John the Baptist, others say Elijah, and others Jeremiah or one of the prophets." He said to them, "But who do you say that I am?" Simon Peter replied, "You are the Christ, the Son of the living God." And Jesus answered him, "Blessed are you, Simon Bar-Jona! For flesh and blood has not revealed this to you, but my Father who is in heaven. And I tell you, you are Peter, and on this rock I will build my church.
—MATTHEW 16:13-18a

● WHENEVER AND WHOEVER OF THE COM-
munity put Matthew's Gospel together, it is
laid down in layers. Materials put in a different
chronological order by other writers are collected
under a topical arrangement in Matthew. The
big question in the mid-section of the Gospel
is, "Who is this?" Its earliest form is the query,
"Is this not the carpenter's son?" And for three
chapters there follows a demonstration of the
validity of the question. The implication everywhere is that the question cannot contain the
answer. There is everywhere the feel that he
is more than this question can answer. Every
incident remembered says he is more. What
sign do you bring, they ask, what evidence
comes with you? What do you give us to
show us you are who you are acting as if you

were? How can we believe the image you give of yourself?

The answer to the question, the rhetorical question, about the carpenter's son begins in a Yes—he is the Carpenter's Son. Jonah is the only sign you get, and it still is the only sign of its end a culture can expect. But the Gospel does not let the question drop there anymore than we can drop it. It continues to hang there, this "Who *is* he?" as a backdrop against which all subsequent action in the Gospel is played out. And, it stays on stage a long, long time. In this lesson we have come to the edge of the topic. The Gospel will here give its own answer to that swinging concern: "Who *is* he?"

How concerned everyone seems with answers. We worry much more about answers than questions. Here the *right* question will get a proper answer, and that is news. Except that Jesus is the *asker,* not the answerer. (How strange if he should turn out to have been the real question all this time instead of the *answer* we so glibly claim to have in our possession.) Up to now the questions have been traveling the other way. The disciples always felt free to question. They learned it from scribes, Pharisees, governors, commoners, aristocrats: What shall we do to have life eternal? When is the kingdom?

Are you that one who should come? When is the end of the age? What is the sign of thy coming? Are you, then, a king? But here Jesus reverses the process and asks the question that Christendom would toss around like a hot plate for six hundred years—the question that is still a splitter of men.

It's at Caesarea—Phillipi. The situation is one of building tension and response. The disciples have been mingling with the roadside crowds. The Master asks—as if he did not know how long this matter would ring like a platter dropped on a stone floor—What are they saying? Who do men say that I am?

Here it is. The introduction of a question whose various answers would bring more schism than any other single concern in Christendom. Here it is—the focal-point question for all the christological heresies. Who was Jesus? From whence did he come? How is he man if he is more than man? Is he really man? How is he God—and man? Did he become Son or has he been eternally Son. If he was made Son—when? Has he two natures? Two substances? Two minds? All the great heresies are here. Men traveled 1,400 miles in the emperors' own carriages on Roman roads to debate this set of questions 1,730-odd years ago. They did this

49

at intervals for 300 years. But at Caesarea none of this business had appeared. They had an easy answer:

> You are John, the Baptizer.
> You are Elijah; You are Jeremiah,
>   some other prophet.

And then the question turns. (They always do when relevant.) In fact, it hadn't even been asked till now:

> But who do *you* say that I am?

Here it is; there is a bold demand implicit here. There is here a thrust, a test, a dividing. He puts it at them. He still does. "Who do *you* say . . . ?" And there is a great silence building up. An answer is demanded to fill this silence. The question rings—it *has* to have answer.

It still does. Luther's cutting cry at this point is devastatingly personal: "I care not whether he be Christ, but that *he be Christ for thee!*"

Unless he is who he is *to you, for you,* he may as well not be who he is. He gets his effective identity in your answer. It is as if he is who you say he is. He *is* who you say to you.

Our lives say who he is to us. The way we live with our kin says who he is to us. Our almost nonexistent outside concerns as a congregation say who he is. Our slums say it. Our hatreds say it. Our real desires say it. Our preoccupations say it. That around which your life really turns says who he is to you. The disreputable fringes of our stewardship have said who he is to us.

And: our high altar, this elevated pulpit, this gracious table of his, these celebrations in this beautiful place; these say who he is, along with our ideals and dreams for our own and his.

If he is who you say, we no longer ask why things are as they are. We already know. Things are as they are because we have said who he is to us and our answer is less than he is. Where, unless at Constantinople in the time of Helena the empress and Chrysostom the preacher, did Christianity ever have a better chance than here. But isn't this a belt of agony around the middle part of our confession as to who he is? If he is who he says, he expects us to do his work and fix it.

Meantime, back at Caesarea, Simon cannot endure the silence. The "Who do *you* say" rings in his ears until he thrusts out an answer:

You? You are the Christ! (The one who would come; the annointed and designated; the endured and endowed.)
The Christ, the Son of the Eternal who lives!

51

Blessed are you, Simon. Flesh and blood have not revealed. . . . Congratulations, Simon: you did not figure this out by yourself. My Father in the heavens has. . . . Congratulations, Simon, you have yourself a revelation . . . a revelation from God about who I am—and this puts you in church (upon this rock . . .). How does it go?

> Congratulations, Simon, you have gotten an insight from God as to who I am and have acted on it and this puts you in church!

It always does. The reaction to who he is puts us in church always. It even says which church we are in. And if your church says Christ is less than Lord, your church is less than church.

Is this deliberate in Matthew's Gospel—this bootlegged notion of the church being sized by its Lord? Of course this is deliberate. This is the point of the whole passage. It is the confessing church of the first century that is putting this together anyhow, and this is the point:

When you say Christ is Lord you are in church, for church is when we say thou art the Christ. And more, church is *how* we say this. Our church reveals the quality of our saying he is Lord, not the quality of his lordship. For to say, on a revelation from the Father, that Christ is truly Lord does things to us.

And now I am telling you, he says, that you are no longer Simon (flat-nose, a hearer); you are Peter (petros, a rock), and on this rock (petra, a ledge [?]) I will be building my church —ecclesia mou—the church of me:

> A conviction within, met by a revelation from God that Jesus is the Son-Redeemer, confessed, puts a man in Church.

This *constitutes* the Church of Christ. This is how you got in, every one of you; for you were somewhere heard to say Christ is Lord. The Epistle of I Peter makes it clear when it says,

> You also are living stones built-up to. . . .

That is to say,

> You also have been put in church by this confession.

And your church is like your Lord, or *vice versa.*

Who do *you* say that he is? If he is Lord to us, really, why is he so lenient with us? If he is Lord, why do some have so much left over and why must others come on Saturday to borrow bread? If he is Lord, how can it cost us so little to enjoy all his beneficence? If he is Lord, how can we be allowed to give so much of our energy to our own station and status? Why are we not in his harness doing his work in some constant field of concern? If he is Lord, why is grace so cheap, so scattered and spotted, so temporary? Why are we so bumbling and inept at changing things? If he is Lord, why is he so weak and ineffectual; why is our church ours and not his; and why are our borders so close and our work so self-centered?

If he is Lord, why, in the more than fifty years since Governor Aycock pushed it down Carolina's throat that she must give her one-third Negro citizenry a fair chance, too, or die, why have we done so little? Why are we 47th in school expenditures, 48th in illiteracy, why are 209 of each 1,000 nonwhites unfit for military service; why are we *47th* in our proportion of educational failures, and why do we have more houses unfit for human animals to hide in than 48 other states?

If he is Lord, where are his lands, his folk, his factories, his schools, his troops, his legislatures, his barns, his stores, his reserves, his projects of change?

If he is Lord, why are our bins so full and his so empty? If he is Lord, where is his artillery?

I have a question. Who do *you* say that he is? Is he Lord at all in the Piedmont?

In North Carolina Christ is a quarter-time Lord.

IV

Lord of the Gates of Death

Simon Peter replied, "You are the Christ, the Son of the living God." And Jesus answered him, "Blessed are you, Simon Bar-Jona! For flesh and blood has not revealed this to you, but my Father who is in heaven. And I tell you, you are Peter, and on this rock I will build my church, and the powers of death shall not prevail against it. I will give you the keys of the kingdom of heaven, and whatever you bind on earth shall be bound in heaven, and whatever you loose on earth shall be loosed in heaven." Then he strictly charged the disciples to tell no one that he was the Christ.

—MATTHEW 16:16-20

● THE INFLUENTIAL FORM-CRITICS OF THE
1930's said that Christ did not *say* these words:

> You are Peter, and on this rock I will
> build my church, and the powers of
> death shall not prevail against it.

It really doesn't matter. The writer of Matthew's
Gospel, the early church, has a point to make,
and these words in their story make that point:
They aim to say in the strongest possible way
that the church made church by this confession
has a great deal of territory to take in.

Whether these are his words or not they
lived their church on their ability to say these
were his words; i.e., their faith-life said that he
takes in this much territory—even beyond the

gates of the dead. This makes the most positive witness available to us as to their conviction about who he is.

I

THE character of the church is *prima facie* evidence of the quality of its confession of its Lord. The character of the church is determined by how much territory its Lord holds in *demesne*. Its Lord's domain is its Lord's control and reveals his character as well. Where the church is a fifth-rate power, its Lord is a fifth-rate Lord. Where the church is a humanist do-gooder, its Lord is the same. Where the church offers only a mild cathartic, this is all its Lord has got. Where the church is a glob of Confederate ideals clinging to the lusty limbs of a secular and cancerous clump, its Lord is a Little Lord Fauntleroy dressed in a narcissism of those ideals. Where the church is spiritless, lost, sidetracked, left behind, conformist, stupid, or blind—so is its Lord. The church is always like its Lord. Those who hear him as a long-ago teacher or prophet get all that a teacher or prophet can give them, but that is all and they ought not to expect more unless their Lord has more.

There is, then, no bigger question than the question, Who is your Lord? What is he like? This question the church always answers in terms of its own character. The political principal by which Germany was divided into Lutheran and Catholic territories applies as well here as anywhere else. *Cuius regio eius religio;* they spelled it out. "Whose the region his the religion." And seventy mighty princes called themselves Lutheran Princes. The same holds here, I say. Whose the region his the religion. Whose the Lordship his the church. Your church is like your Lord.

II

Look how much territory they took in at Caesarea when their church was defined by the character of *their* Lord. These writers, or this writer, who reflect the judgment and experience of the early church with Christ—they weren't fooling around!

> You are a rock and on this rock I
> will build my church and the powers
> of death shall not prevail against it!

Now this could be a bigger church than you meant to join. It takes in a lot of territory.

This is no mere womb to tomb affair with something special for every age-group. Its outside bound is bigger than life-size. Its bounding strength under its mighty Lord is such that it even takes in hell itself. Ought not this to tell us who he is?

Whatever they may hold against the mighty Roman Catholic Church where you grew up, its vice never did lie in its taking in too little territory! Whomever the pope may represent in Rome, it's not a lesser Lord over a part of life. And even though there are those who have said in jest (the joke is over a hundred years old) that the pope has got so out of hand that God is *his* assistant in heaven, the early church and the Roman Catholic Church have taken seriously that the size Lord they have requires a lot of territory. In that Roman Church he holds domain over birth and death, marriage and mind, law and government, the cities of earth, the sex mores, certain property regulations, the sin and the private thoughts, the kings and the princes, the navies and armies, the lesser lords and lands and laws: *All* are provincial to the church. Its church is its Lord's domain! Even down to hell and here the gates of the land of the departed cannot keep it out.

How much territory does your church control?

Or as Napoleon once put it, "how many legions
has the Pope?" What is the strength of your
Lord's artillery? This is the question you have
answered. Your Lord is the strength and scope
of your church.

Only the true character of his Lordship when
properly confessed justifies so fantastic a claim as
this. He is no mere carpenter's son, they are
saying. His Lordship extends even over death,
for we know him resurrected. They were not
saying that the church would defeat the forces
of hell in every encounter. They were not saying
Evil had been put out of business. They were
not saying that in any combat it has the church
would always win. They were not even saying
that the church on earth would always be on
the good side of things. They were saying, in
the light of their experience with him, in his
resurrection, that even the land beyond life
did not lie outside his dominion and would not
see cut off the relationships he had established.
They were saying that since he is who he is
there is no bound to his territory. He can claim
it all—and this is a different matter.

How much territory must faith now give
him? Is it not possible he is just like everything else we overvalue or undervalue? Isn't
the truth most likely to be found somewhere in

between these extremes of carpenter's son and Son of God? I think not: Christ is Lord or a fool. There's no real in-between available for us. Even the self-styled Anti-Christ, Friedrich Nietzsche knew this. But do not take his self-accusation seriously without knowing that he signed two late letters "The Crucified."

To Nietzsche Jesus was a case of "delayed puberty." In *Thus Spake Zarathustra,* the old man says: "He died too early; he himself would have recanted his teaching had he reached my age." Nietzsche describes Jesus as having endurance beyond belief, but as being completely indifferent to advantage. Jesus had serenity but not self-control, for there was nothing to be controlled, since he lived in a state of freedom from all passion.

He does not resist, he does not defend his right, he takes no step which might ward off the worst; on the contrary, he provokes it. And he begs, he suffers, he loves with those, in those who do him evil. [He teaches] not to resist, not to be angry, not to hold responsible, to resist not even the evil one, but to love him.

Such a Lord is deluded and a fool, a passionless, prepuberty holdover who has no place in this jungle world—

Or: He knew of and believed in, is committed to and already living within, a realm that so far transcends our animal existence as to make its fretting agonies of no consequence.

He is Lord of all or not Lord at all. Which? You say. Your answer is the character of your church.

The only way he and his followers could effectively say who he was is by the territory they claimed to be under his dominion. So they took it all—even death. It was like Balboa seeing the Pacific from the Isthmus of Panama, and, with no notion of the size of his claim, he took it all and all its shores for Spain.

III

HAVE you been subtly swallowed by that terribly ubiquitous temptation to believe that this life is all there is? That death is unbridgeable; that the grave is a dead end? That we must come to terms with "this" as being all there is? Is this why we seek so frantically, in Harry Golden's words, to "enjoy, enjoy"?

This may well be so for most of us, especially in our darker moments. But if we do this, we cannot do it from within the Church of the Christ. The Church of the Lord Christ *began* by dealing with that enemy farthest out or closest up, as your case may be. It dealt at first and at one with death: The Lord's death and its own death. And who is he now? This is a new dimension. If he is *this* sort of Lord, if he is, as the ancients said, *Pontifex Maximus,* the supreme bridge-builder, and if his church includes the land across the river where there are trees, and if his church includes us, what closer ground does he aim for us to inhabit?

He aims for us to conquer every social agony between *here* where we are and *there* where his boundary is undimmed by our frequent dyings.

My friend at the publishing house insisted that the little book on the seven last words of Christ should be closed with a sermon on Resurrection, since it was for Eastertime. But it was one of those times when I hardly knew how to receive or believe this great wonder, so I used the text:

"Behold, I show you a mystery."

The following week, the week of the assassination of that young and fair chief of ours, I was forced to my knees in gratitude that there was another text, even then being sung in Latin words in a pontifical requiem mass:

"We do not grieve as men who have no hope, for since we believe that Jesus . . . "

And in the months since I have been able to hear some other texts too: That one so dear to old Karl Barth,

"every eye shall see him"

and that one we hear sung even in Advent, and much more so at Holy Week:

King of Kings, Lord of Lords!

And the one I just read where he says in the Revelation of St. John,

"I am Alpha and Omega, the beginning and the end,
I will give unto him that is athirst. . . . "

But so, for me, beyond in the midst of the mystery, he keeps calling that he will build his church which isn't cut off even by the gates of death, and it is for those to whom he is Lord.

V

The
Gospel
Contradiction

FROM that time Jesus began to show his disciples that he must go to Jerusalem and suffer many things from the elders and chief priests and scribes, and be killed, and on the third day be raised. And Peter took him and began to rebuke him, saying, "God forbid, Lord! This shall never happen to you." But he turned and said to Peter, "Get behind me, Satan! You are a hindrance to me; for you are not on the side of God, but of men."

—MATTHEW 16:21-23

● WHY CAN THE BELIEVER NOT SETTLE ONCE for all the Jesus question? Why does this concern about who he is keep constantly recurring? Why do we not dispose of this God-man scandal? This stumbling-block in incarnation, can it not be dispensed with?

You started with "Is he not the carpenter's son with his sign of Jonah?" We had no trouble seeing him as human. But, as soon as we accepted that, you switched. Your narrative and sermons built up to the claim that he is *more* than a carpenter. We heard the great confession —thou Christ, the Son of the God who lives! With this-sized Lord we found ourselves in a church that takes in a vast territory—the gates of the land of death. We have received this by faith as best we can. Why do you not now drop the question where we were able to say, "He is Lord"?

The answer? Jesus himself, in *Matthew's Gospel*, will not drop it there. The very moment his Lordship is revealed there is seen, against the backdrop of that great confession, a terrible contradiction: He begins to prepare them for a Cross! The confession will not lie still. It surges back and forth between his manhood and his Godhood. What does this mean?

As a matter of fact, had you not noticed how all the Gospel narratives feature a set of built-in surges? There is a series of careening lunges from left to right. There is a wild sequence of cascades—he is up—he is down. The Gospel is split by a mighty contradiction. It's as if we have two irreconcilables in the same bucket.

Confessed as Lord, he says immediately, using a different name for himself, that the Son of man goes up to Jerusalem to die. "Christ is Lord!" they say. He says, "Tell nobody!" He feeds the five thousand, then takes a boat overnight to escape the kingdom they wish to thrust upon him. The rich young ruler seeks and leaves dejected over the rejection of his attendant kingdom. The Teacher dines with an aristocrat but talks to a harlot who had wandered by. Born to be king, he has the air of a peasant. To his coronation he rides a donkey.

In this lesson, look, he deliberately leads them through a claim, its opposite, and a new resolution. It's the pattern of Hegelian dialectic! Thesis—antithesis—synthesis—then destroys the synthesis in a new dialectic:

"Who do men say that I am?

You are Moses or one of the prophets. (*thesis*)

But who do you say that I am?

Thou art the Christ, Son of the living God." (*antithesis*)

(It's as if he had reached into Simon Peter and turned on an explosively opposite answer.)

Then the *synthesis:* Congratulations, Peter, your confession has marked out a boundary for a church bigger than death. What a resolution. Why cannot we stop it there at this glorious synthesis of manhood and godhood? The size of your Lord is the size of your church. It's a good place to stop. But notice the old pattern emerge. Instead of staying with this synthesis of confession, the synthesis is broken and turned into a new beginning. It becomes a bucking, yawing timber in a high sea looking for its opposite to form a new dialectic.

This begins in the thesis: Your church has a

73

Lord forever! Then the disquieting antithesis
again: But he must die!

I

SIMON, the original confessor who kicked off
this recognition business, simply cannot stand
this. This contradiction is more than he could
take. (Later, wouldn't it break Peter open to
learn that a man could love and deny, believe
and disobey and break his heart all in the same
breath?)

He had just been given a Lord, a standing,
an assurance, an acceptance forever! He cannot
stand the contradictions. He wants his confessed
recognition of Messiah to stand pat. He wants
no wavering, no inconsistency. He wants no
yawing of contradictory ideas in these high
seas. But he now hears Jesus say:

> The Son of man goes up to
> Jerusalem to be crucified.

And that ruins everything!

Lord! he cries, be this far from you!

May this *never* come to you!

(Was not Peter the one with the knife in the
garden at Olivet?) Keep this Lordship where
it belongs—on the up and up! The Lordship is
settled; let it settle things!

And all he gets for this is the most terrible personal rebuke the Lord ever delivered. The Lord now says to his prime confessor:

Get behind me, Satan; you are an offense
    to me.
Get behind me, Adversary; you are a stumbl-
    ing block.
Go down, Satanos; you are a scandal, a
    trap, a threat to break my back.
Hush, Simon: you are a scandal to my scan-
    dal; you are a threat to the Cross!

It's a gentle rebuke, however, for how could poor Simon have known? 'Tis an agony six centuries of debate could not quiet. To confess him as son of a carpenter and as Son of God requires the absorption of a mighty contradiction. This is the problem: He *is* man and he *is* Lord.

II

No confession of Christ as Lord is proper if it makes him not a man. No confession of Christ as man is proper if it makes him not the Lord. Our confession has to take in a lot of territory. It has to allow for the *humanity of God,* and this is impossible. It has to allow for the Godhood of humanity, and this is almost unprintable. It strains us. We cannot easily allow so much of goodness, or grandeur, or stature to man. Will a man rob God!

The New Testament does. The Lord hath reigned—from the tree. The Messiah of Israel —has a carpenter's adz in his hand. The Son of God—has feet that need washing. "I and the Father are One"—and Jesus wept. The Lamb of God—with its throat cut. It's a dramatic and agonizing contradiction. That man is so much more than we thought; that God is so much more human than we dreamed; who can take it in? In Louis Nizer's *A Case of Libel* the lawyer puts the Christ on the witness stand and asks if it is true that he consorted with harlots, sinners, and publicans, that he was a wine-bibber and a glutton. And he is guilty. It is so. He takes in this much territory and so do his followers. If we deny him this he calls us a scandal and a denier of his selfhood and tells us to get behind him.

It is gospel true, but it is a split true. He takes in all this territory. And man? The New Testament requires of us an agonized stretch to take in man's potential as revealed in The Man. So much to man; so near he is to God. The contradictions buck and plunge in the sea of our minds. So much man; so much God. Who can resolve our split confession? No one, not even the New Testament writers; this splitness hangs there unless:

The gospel contradiction is gospel incarnation. This is the only reconciling out we have. Incarnation. When God is God so much that it overleaps the Godhood, then man can become so much man that it overleaps the manhood. The effect is an overlap: God-man; the manhood of God; the Godhood of man. They belong together! They, God and man always did belong together; since creation they have belonged to each other. This is the real *Imago Dei*. And it means that given this view of the field both our potential and our present actuality take in much more territory than we know. The least of us is much more powerful. The man of of us is much more Godly. The God of us is much more manly. We have more room than we have used. We are closer to God than we thought.

In the Christian gospel this closeness to God, this incarnation, imposes a terrible burden upon us—the burden of real manhood. At a conference on race problems this year, A. J. Ryan said that he had discovered that the burden of being a man was enough! He could no longer carry the load of having to be a black or white one in addition. Just to be man is enough. A man cannot carry *all* this manhood with its adjectives. And, he cannot carry his Godhood at all unless there is really a *new human race.* And how is this new race of men—these men of Godhood—put together and constituted?

III

WATCH this Gospel swing back immediately from that crest. Really, it is incredible the way this Gospel yaws back and forth.

Peter undoubtedly was crushed by our Lord's rebuke. Battered by the contradiction, silenced, he stands there utterly hang-jawed. So, next paragraph, the Lord, after six days of this, takes Peter with James and John and goes apart into "an high mountain." And there, before the shattered Simon, the old versions say his countenance was changed, he was transfigured until he *glistered;* and, to their complete amazement it was as it had been at the baptism. A voice said, "This is the Son."

Then—there appear *Moses* and *Elijah!* Everybody who matters is there. Everyone who ever mattered is there except Abraham and he was busy holding Lazarus in his bosom. Peter sees it: When Christ is in his glory only Moses and Elijah are fit to talk with him! Good Lord! he cries, something has run together here. Manhood and Godhood have run together and it is unforgettable! Let us build *three* tabernacles —three tents of meeting. One for you, one for Moses, and one for Elijah!

And now, here, what more is there left us to see and confess of this mighty contradiction?

After two thousand years we still have to say that something mighty has run into revelation here before our very eyes. Two irreconcilables, manhood and Godhood, are met in a single container to where one is the other. One who is like us is so unlike us as to reveal to us a whole vast unclaimed territory for a new human race. One of us has appeared among us in such a way as to reveal our Godliness. There are rooms upstairs we have never entered!

And so there are. But their occupancy is no ordinary matter. A man has to lay *claim* to them. For do you not remember how the Gospel yaws again? At the foot of Mt. Transfiguration a father, bearing his epileptic in his arms, runs to meet Messiah crying—Lord, if you can do anything. . . . And he answers—all manhood is possible to the believer.

Lord, I believe—Help thou mine unbelief.

In John Updike's sensitive first novel, *The Poorhouse Fair,* Conner, the director of the poor farm has succeeded in tearing out the ground for faith upon which several old timers had relied as they gathered around a smoky fireplace. Conner's overt need to establish his own brand of humanism had swept him recklessly over their poor and timid objections. Presently, old man Hook, a ninety-four-year-old pauper schoolteacher speaks:

"Let an old fella say one thing more and then he'll hold his peace. When you get to be my age—and I shall pray that you never do—I wish it on no one, but if you do—you shall know this: There is no goodness, without belief. There is nothing but busyness. And if you have not believed, at the end of your life you shall know you have buried your talent in the ground of this world and have nothing saved to take into the next."

VI
Your
Own
Cross

THEN Jesus told his disciples, "If any man would come after me, let him deny himself and take up his cross and follow me. For whoever would save his life will lose it, and whoever loses his life for my sake will find it. For what will it profit a man, if he gains the whole world and forfeits his life? Or what shall a man give in return for his life? For the Son of man is to come with his angels in the glory of his Father, and then he will repay every man for what he has done. Truly, I say to you, there are some standing here who will not taste death before they see the Son of man coming in his kingdom."

—MATTHEW 16:24-28

● How DOES THIS REVERSED GOSPEL—THIS gospel of my Godhood get to me? What is the Christian connection that involves me?

"I care not whether he be Christ, but that he be Christ for *thee!*"

Now how does this get to me? How does this recognition of Lord-Christ matter? Where do we get connected with the lordliness? Where does this water hit my wheel? How does it make any difference who Christ is—how is it that the Lord and I are related? What is the tie-in to my life?

I

IT IS all a matter of *recognition,* some say. Not so, that would be a passing matter—no more than to say, "I saw him once, but nothing passed between us." It is more. To be connected to Jesus Christ is a matter of *believing*, they say Peter said in his sermons. But for me, for us, this apparently simple matter of believing on hearsay from behind us has been so difficult as to be nearly impossible. It is really all a matter of *adoption* on the initiative of the Father, without any responsibility or competency on my own part, they say Paul said—and "they" say and have said much more:

Most simply you heard it said, "only believe" (that Jesus is the Son of God). Just put your mind to it—or better assent and lay your mind aside—no problems really. There is nothing to be lost and everything to be gained; and besides, there is so little demanded, no high obedience, no penetrating involvement, and just a surface ethic of easy conformity. Come! Whoever you are or were, only believe—and by hundreds of thousands they have come; but nothing has changed or been changed by their coming— even the comers.

Or next, and perhaps even more comfortably, they say we are connected to Christ in an heraldic or familial fashion, according to who one's family has been in an ageless and beautiful *covenant relation*. Lived out, deeply and seriously, in a closed society where the majority belong and families are mostly *in,* who can deny that it makes a gracious, reputable manhood and a vibrant, even colorful sociality of those who eat, drink, make, and want the same things. Charming, really, in its older cultural settings, but this excludes so very many.

Yet, and as for those whose exigencies of birth leave them outside the covenantal heritage, there is the way indispensable for all, the way of organic church connection with the only real Church there is, the institution blessed of and founded by its Lord. Meet its initiation requirements, attend its classes, adopt its ideology, and you are in—for without it no one really belongs, and, as for those who have this, who can say!

There have always been those among Christians who feel more is required of us for salvation than these. The first notion (only believe) is beefed up and made to be, in the lingo, *a responsible decision about Jesus.* Or those who want more for a covenantal connection decorate it with *a creedal and catechetical competence;* the work of years in parish and church school classes and endless drilling (in earlier times) by devout grandmothers. And as for salvation by organic connection, this is endlessly extended in meaning by *a ritual induction* that began near birth with a baptism not complete until so-called confirmation years later, or postponed (since God's gracious withholding can be counted on for eight or so years in most cases) until time for a so-called responsible or adult baptism (of a child!), as if any baptism could ever have more than a prospective meaning, a meaning to be apprehended later and as one goes.

Over and beyond all this, the simplest way to one's salvation is the way of dogmatic assent, acceptance of and agreement with the whole body of teaching, however contrived or put together. So eager becomes the desire to include it all, that rank on rank, one behind the other, the great creeds march over consecutive pages in the Prayer-Book: the Apostles' Creed, bristling with its addenda to that simple apostolic "Christ is Lord"; then the Nicene, with all its Greek distinctions so superfluous to life itself; and then, that gorgeous omnibus for faith, the Athanasian Creed, read by few, remembered by some, and recited by almost none, but there.

Under all this, just as brittle, even more authoritarian, shaped like a mathematical equation, a veritable geometry of guaranteed salvation is developed from Pauline writings by people who have mostly missed the point. As rigidly as any calculus, it goes in its prescribed order of experience: conviction of *sin*, confession of *sin*, repentance for *sin*, turning to *Christ*, confession of *Christ*, acceptance by *Christ*, then baptism.

Nine ways of salvation? Incredible—and it really is unbelievable. In fact, this is what's wrong with them; they are mostly unbelievable. Actually, the "nine ways" are three: (1) Salvation is by *fait accompli,* a closed transaction. (2) Salvation is a dispensation, a doled-out favor from God through the church. (3) Salvation is an accomplishment, the work of one's lifetime and longer. All these are ways of *connecting* us with the Christ. Some are a result of mishearing and are antithetical to the gospel and to humanity. Some have great and grave truths buried within and between them. Is it possible that lying under all these sophisticated methodologies of redemption there is an *earlier mode of experience?* I believe we have this, and that we have it here in Matthew's Gospel: a way that evades completely that ungodly preoccupation with the self and its destiny which characterizes all the ways we have heard so far. And more, it is the way the early church found it that they were related to Christ.

II

To THE early communities relation to Christ was simply *a coming after*. How sad that the renovaters of Christian experience have made such a formidable and complex theology of salvation.

(I carry on a sporadic correspondence with a private priest of mine, one-time passionist and teacher of repute in the Roman Catholic Church. From his last, this is relevant, if not utterly annihilating, to most of our notions of "salvation":

Any use of analogy, my dear theologian, is a fair measure of one's ignorance, but it is an invaluable asset to you whose business it is to tell others how to think and talk about God.

If I were God in a mood about to destroy this blatant planet, I'd begin with all the theologians and complete my blessed work in peace and quiet. God is God because He is like *me!* And I am an I because of my likeness to Him! We are both under the necessity of being ourselves and God [and I] respect nothing more than the *person*. If God had not done this, to say it would be blasphemous insolence!)

I am to be an I; I am like God. The early church recognized here a profoundly relational identification, and they knew how it would come about—and, as Sam, my private Jew, says when reading the Scriptures to me, "here comes the business!"

"If any will come after me let him deny himself, take up his cross, and follow me."

There is just no way to get away from this.

If *any*: it is all-inclusive; no heraldry or familial or tribal considerations here—if any, man, woman, child; any! This is Hocking's *universal*. He calls the "if any" (though in another place, namely the "if any will open the door" in Revelation) the most *inclusive* word in the gospel, and the word that makes it real gospel!

Will come after: most simply put means, if any can stand God at his elbow, can endure the identification of God and man.

Let him deny himself: not deny himself something he wants—there's no direct object here —but simply let himself deny himself—deny his images of the self, deny his ideas of himself, deny his self-concepts, deny his own ends. Let him submit to the correction of his self-images by the image of God as man.

Take up his cross: and here the text breaks down and we are in trouble. The phrase is not

89

in Mark's Gospel, our earliest, and we are saved, thank God! The Christian life can dispense with crosses. Mark, in the newly found manuscript (Codex 2427), simply does not have the word about our own crosses. And this may be our most significant point. Mark doesn't have it, and Mark didn't say it; but later Matthew does say it! The church found out in its own body that it had to add it—that those who "came after" carried crosses too. (Indeed, says a Jewish general, the Romans ran out of wood for crosses, crosses for bodies, and ground on which to put crosses, but not out of bodies for crosses, in the midst of Titus' last phase against the upper city of Jerusalem in 70-73 (A.D.) And the church knew soon enough that all had their crosses. Mark or no, they had to add it.

And follow: not *imitatio,* but *sequentia.* There is no way to get away from this. The relation to Jesus is not a conferred blessing, not an acquired or bestowed status. It is not a differentiation of quality nor a "better than," but it is a simple relation of following. What it means "to come after," to "deny self," to "take up your death," "to follow"; these meanings are the real content of our gospel.

III

IF COLLINGWOOD, a representative philosopher on this point, is right at all, the new world view requires us to put structure and function together. Structure is being, function is doing, and being-doing are aspects of the same reality. That is to say, in older terminology, faith has always been more than believing. What one believes out of what one is, is what one does. Faith is belief that obeys and to be Christian is inseparable from the demand to do Christ. Faith is that believing the doing of which is such that the do-er can stand God at his elbow. This is to follow—it is identification.

How can there be self-forgiveness for the discrepancy between our confession and our practice? If this earlier notion of relation with Christ is so—then is it not a responsibility that concerns where our living goes? There is involved Christianly what we have fought for, treasured, ached to get, diverted with, ignored, passed by, refused to see; *plus* the terribly casual way we walk by death, our easy loving and leave-taking, and the still easier way in which religion becomes both pattern and a patter.

Really, there simply is no other way to get connected with this gospel than to get involved. To be *there*, where one is, is to be with it:

the Cross gets *to* you. And the Cross is not burdens, or frustrations, or even limitations; nor is it necessarily your violent death, but it does include the matter that we have to die.

What is that cross here with us? What had that early church discovered that made them predict cross for us, too?

The relation to Christ, the meaning of our atonement, the risk one runs to have God at his elbow, the inevitable concomitant of our salvation means that at this cross *there is no place for observers*. There is no detached ground; there are no uninvolved ones. We are caught *here*. Cross means nailed *here*. There are no spectators. The "divinity of the spectator" has disappeared. We are all "on stage." You are in it: the drama for the redemption of the world. But not alone—there are no single crosses anywhere, anymore. All our crosses participate in his. And by the same token, this means that there is no way of evasion open to us. Our only choice is as to whether our suffering finiteness is unto life or unto death. We all face the

little boxes, little boxes.

When the church put Matthew's Gospel together out of its memories, they had discovered some deeper matters about how their own crosses participate in the cross of God's Son. This surely must explain why they added the phrase "take up his cross."

How God would do what he would do involves my own enfleshing of God; my personal revealing of what God is like. I have to endure God at my elbow. William Temple and George Buttrick have already made the same connection in similar language, but what is meant is that if men say that a good God would be heartbroken by our human situation the Cross-Christian answers, "See my sorrow." If God cared he would carry our load, they say, but we answer, "See us carrying." Or if they say that a loving God would *do*, the only answer God has got is our own doing. "See us doing." That is to say, this relation makes us demonstrations of the power of God, and this is why God's power is no determinism but rather an accommodation. Precisely because God's power is accommodated and not an operative determinism, what God does in his people can slip back; but for the eight hundred years behind us the trail is clear. We can see where man is headed—toward the fulfillment of his manhood, his personhood, his humanity. He has become God's power to do where he is related.

All of which means that our cross is our way to live connected. The higher self is "lost" in the lower; not vice versa. This is why it is called "losing one's life." *One lays down his life in the service of the lower;* a reversal of the usual Christian injunction. But the direction of Incarnation is always toward the lower. One does, to reverse the injunction in *Streetcar Named Desire,* one does "go back with the beasts" in order to save. He interposes himself, he gets in the line-up, he associates with transgressors for the transgressors. He discovers his own ultimate concern in medicine, or race problems, or poverty, or ignorance, or motherhood, or some trusteeship by being healer, curer, teacher, mother, redeemer. He cares—utterly, that is, ultimately.

This week, with a new mother, second baby, came one of those great moments when she raised, then answered, the question about the meaning of her travail.

"Not pain," she said, "but concern."
Exactly. It is *Da Sein:* to be there, involved, where one is, unable to be away from *there,* where one is, impaled. Birthing is a crucifixion —and crucifixion is a birthing of a life stretched out to show what God is like. Some suicides require thirty years to finish, and some cruci-

fixions take longer, but we do have that choice between suffering that is death and suffering that gives life.

Some "theologians" laugh at me for this, but you do become Christ. That emotional, erratic, imprecise Greek-Russian Berdyaev is right. I become a Redeemer, the only one some ever see. Is this not what breaks on Paul when he cries:

"I am crucified with Christ, yet not I, for
Christ liveth in me!"

It runs together with the experience of the ancient community of faith—

If any
will come after me,
let him deny himself,
take up his cross,
and follow.

This gospel-in-our-experience we will not let you forget. If any preaches any other gospel to you let him be Anathema.